Cuttlefish

A Buddy Book by
Deborah Coldiron

ABDO
Publishing Company

UNDERWATER
WORLD

VISIT US AT
www.abdopublishing.com

Published by ABDO Publishing Company, 8000 West 78th Street, Edina, Minnesota 55439.

Coordinating Series Editor: Sarah Tieck
Contributing Editor: Michael P. Goecke
Graphic Design: Deborah Coldiron
Cover Photograph: Photos.com
Interior Photographs/Illustrations: Brandon Cole Marine Photography (pages 9, 11, 25); Clipart.com (page 15); Corbis (page 18); Image Quest Marine: Roger Steene (page 23), James D. Watt (page 23); ImageMix (page 28); Minden Pictures: Fred Bavendam (pages 7, 17, 21), Hans Leijnse (page 30); Photos.com (pages 5, 10, 12, 13, 18, 19, 27, 29)

Library of Congress Cataloging-in-Publication Data

Coldiron, Deborah.
    Cuttlefish / Deborah Coldiron.
      p. cm. -- (Underwater world)
    Includes index.
    ISBN 978-1-60453-132-9
    1. Cuttlefish--Juvenile literature. I. Title.

QL430.3.S47C65 2008
594'.58 -- dc22

2008005046

Table Of Contents

The World Of Cuttlefish

Every living creature needs water. Some animals not only need water, they live in it, too.

Scientists have found more than 250,000 kinds of plants and animals living underwater. And, they believe there could be one million more! The cuttlefish is one animal that makes its home in this underwater world.

Water covers 70 percent of Earth's surface.

The cuttlefish has a soft body and many arms. The smallest cuttlefish are about one inch (3 cm) long. The largest may be five feet (2 m) in length.

The giant cuttlefish is the world's largest cuttlefish species. It is found near Australia.

There are about 100 cuttlefish **species** in our underwater world. Cuttlefish live in shallow **tropical** and **temperate** waters in most areas of the world. But, they are not found off the coasts of North, Central, or South America.

Cuttlefish live near the seafloor.

A Closer Look

Cuttlefish are not actually fish. They are **mollusks**. Other mollusks include snails, clams, octopuses, and squid.

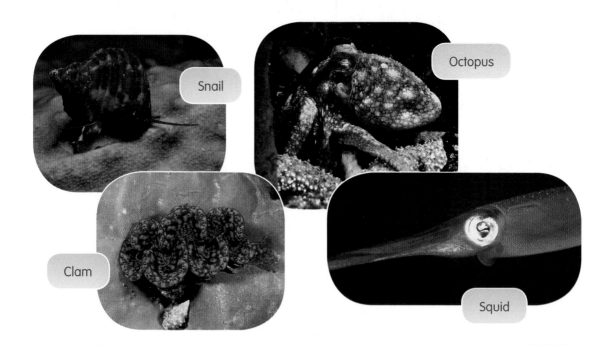

Snail

Octopus

Clam

Squid

Cuttlefish do not see color. But, they have very good eyesight.

A cuttlefish has two large eyes with W-shaped **pupils**. Its many arms surround its mouth. The mouth has a pair of beaklike jaws for eating prey.

The main part of a cuttlefish's body is its mantle. On either side of its mantle is a long fin. Fins help the cuttlefish move forward, backward, and even in circles.

Cuttlefish have called Earth's oceans home for more than 21 million years.

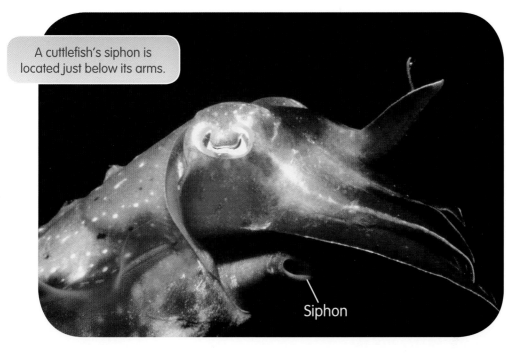

A cuttlefish's siphon is located just below its arms.

Siphon

To move quickly, a cuttlefish takes water into its mantle. Then, it forces the water out through a tube called a siphon (SEYE-fuhn). This moves the cuttlefish backward at great speed.

FAST FACTS

Squid and octopuses also use siphons to push themselves through the water.

15

Cuttlefish have eight arms and two long feeding **tentacles**. Cuttlefish use their tentacles to grab food. Suckers line the arms and the tentacles.

Cuttlefish have a hard inner shell called a cuttlebone. It has tiny holes like a sponge. The cuttlebone helps the cuttlefish control whether it sinks or floats.

The Body Of A Cuttlefish

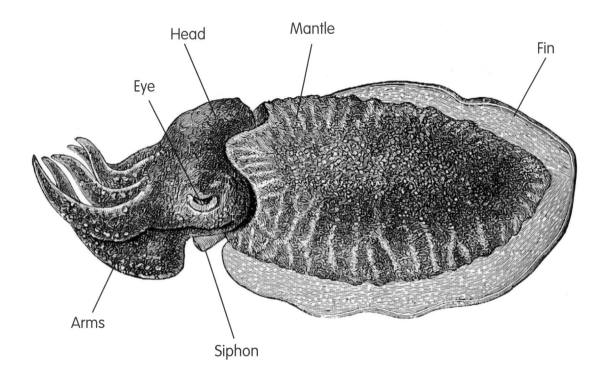

Head

Mantle

Fin

Eye

Arms

Siphon

The two feeding tentacles are not visible. They are hidden inside pouches near the eyes.

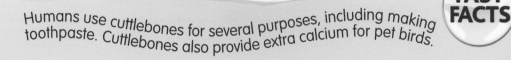

Humans use cuttlebones for several purposes, including making toothpaste. Cuttlebones also provide extra calcium for pet birds.

A Growing Cuttlefish

Cuttlefish mainly reproduce in spring and summer. Females lay 100 to 300 eggs. Cuttlefish eggs take about four months to hatch.

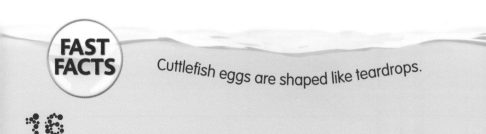

FAST FACTS

Cuttlefish eggs are shaped like teardrops.

Cuttlefish females find safe hiding places for their eggs to develop and hatch.

Cuttlefish have short life spans. Most live for about 18 months. Females die shortly after laying eggs.

Family Connections

Cuttlefish belong to a group of animals called cephalopods (SEH-fuh-luh-pahds). Cephalopods have soft bodies and many arms. They are some of the most intelligent creatures in the sea.

There are around 800 known cephalopod **species**. This group includes octopuses, nautiluses, and squid.

Octopuses are famous for their ability to squeeze through tiny spaces. They can fit through holes as small as their hard beak.

Octopuses have eight arms and no feeding tentacles.

Unlike other cephalopods, nautiluses have a hard outer shell. Some have as many as 90 arms! But, their arms do not have suckers.

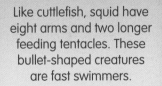

Like cuttlefish, squid have eight arms and two longer feeding tentacles. These bullet-shaped creatures are fast swimmers.

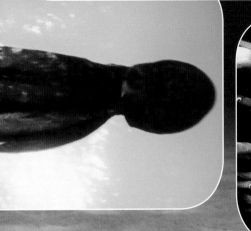

Many squid species travel together in large groups called shoals.

Dinnertime

Cuttlefish eat **mollusks** and **crustaceans** (kruhs-TAY-shuhns). They also eat small fish, **marine** worms, and even other cuttlefish.

Cuttlefish are clever and creative predators. They use a variety of methods to catch prey. Often, they change the look and feel of their skin. Cuttlefish are master hiders!

Cuttlefish use their feeding tentacles to grab prey. When not in use, these tentacles hide inside pouches behind the eyes.

Cuttlefish sneak up on prey. Divers have seen cuttlefish pretend to be coral. Their skin takes on the coral's color and feel. And, their arms form branching shapes, like coral.

If that fails, cuttlefish can put on an amazing light show. Their skin flashes light and dark patterns. This confuses and stuns their prey.

FAST FACTS

Cuttlefish usually hunt for food at night and hide by day. Scientists say they have excellent night vision.

In just seconds, a broadclub cuttlefish can change its skin's feel and appearance *(above)* and then flash lights *(right)*. Scientists say cuttlefish have unlimited colors and patterns to use!

Cuttlefish owe their color-changing abilities to **chromatophores** (kroh-MA-tuh-fawrs). These special **cells** contain colors and reflect light. Cuttlefish have more than 20 million chromatophores.

FAST FACTS

Most cuttlefish use a poison to help them kill their prey. They deliver the poison with a bite from their strong beak. The poison makes the cuttlefish's prey unable to move.

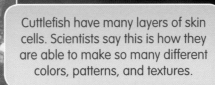

Cuttlefish have many layers of skin cells. Scientists say this is how they are able to make so many different colors, patterns, and textures.

A World Of Danger

The world is an unsafe place for cuttlefish. Dolphins, seals, and many fish eat them. Some cuttlefish even eat other cuttlefish!

Luckily, cuttlefish have several ways to defend themselves from attack. They can release a cloud of ink. Or, they can change the look and feel of their skin. This helps them hide from predators.

FAST FACTS

Cuttlefish can mask their escape with an ink cloud in the water. Some even shoot out bubbles of ink. This confuses enemies and helps cuttlefish escape.

Sharks are cuttlefish predators.

Fascinating Facts

The flamboyant cuttlefish is like no other known cuttlefish. This small creature walks on its fins instead of swimming. It is slow, brightly colored, and one of the most poisonous sea creatures!

Flamboyant cuttlefish

🦑 Cuttlefish ink is known as sepia ink. It was once used by artists and writers.

🦑 Cuttlefish blood is a bluish green color.

🦑 Cuttlefish have enormous brains for their body size.

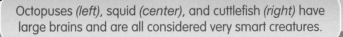

Octopuses *(left)*, squid *(center)*, and cuttlefish *(right)* have large brains and are all considered very smart creatures.

Learn And Explore

Scientists have seen up to 11 male giant cuttlefish compete for one female. So, **marine** biologists are studying the tricks males play on their rivals.

The smaller males pretend to be females and sneak past the larger males. This allows them to get closer to the females!

Some of the smallest giant cuttlefish males disguise themselves. This helps improve their chances of mating.

IMPORTANT WORDS

cell the extremely small basic unit of living matter of which all plants and animals are made.

crustacean any of a group of animals with hard shells that live mostly in water. Crabs, lobsters, and shrimp are all crustaceans.

marine of or relating to the sea.

mollusk an animal with a soft, unsegmented body without a backbone. Snails, clams, and squid are all mollusks.

pupil the opening in the center of the iris of the eye. Light passes through the pupil.

species living things that are very much alike.

temperate having neither very hot or very cold weather.

tentacle a long, slender body part that grows around the mouth or the head of some animals.

tropical having warm temperatures.

WEB SITES

To learn more about cuttlefish, visit ABDO Publishing Company on the World Wide Web. Web sites about cuttlefish are featured on our Book Links page. These links are routinely monitored and updated to provide the most current information available.

www.abdopublishing.com

INDEX